T0288685

AAM gratefully acknowledges the generous financial
support for the Museums & Community Initiative provided by
The Wallace Reader's Digest Funds.

Additional support was received from
The Ford Foundation,
The John S. and James L. Knight Foundation,
and The Nathan Cummings Foundation.

The mission of the American Association of Museums (AAM) is to represent the American museum community, address its needs, and enhance its ability to serve the public. AAM disseminates information on current standards and best practices and provides professional development for staff to ensure that museums contribute to public education in its broadest sense and protect and preserve our cultural heritage.

Since its founding in 1906, AAM has grown to more than 15,900 members, including over 11,000 museum professionals and trustees, 1,900 corporate members, and 3,000 museums.

A Museums & Community Toolkit (a companion publication to Mastering Civic Engagement: A Challenge to Museums)

Copyright © 2002, American Association of Museums, 1575 Eye St. N.W., Suite 400, Washington, DC 20005; www.aam-us.org. All rights reserved. This book may not be reproduced, in whole or in part, in any form, except for brief passages by reviewers, without written permission from the publisher.

Design: LevineRiederer Design

Library of Congress Cataloging-in-Publication Data
A museums & community toolkit.
   p. cm.
 ISBN 0-931201-82-9 (pbk.)
 1. Museums—United States—Management. 2. Museums—United
States—Planning. 3. Museums—Social aspects—United States. 4.
Community development—United States. I. Title: Museums and community
toolkit. II. American Association of Museums.

AM11 .M725 2002
069'.1—dc21

               2002014278

A Museums & Community

TOOLKIT

A Museums & Community
TOOLKIT

Museums & Community

AMERICAN ASSOCIATION OF MUSEUMS

© 2002 American Association of Museums
1575 Eye St. N.W., Suite 400
Washington, DC 20005

TABLE OF CONTENTS
. . . .

INVOLVING THE COMMUNITY

. . . .

By Kim Igoe

Every year, more and more people visit the Tradescant Rose Botanical Gardens. "We need to expand," cries the director, with visions of a new botanical complex (roads and parking included) dancing in her head. "Yes, let's expand," say the trustees, who launch a successful fund-raising campaign to make the vision a reality. But when word of the expansion plans leak out, the garden's neighbors revolt. Soon people with pickets are stationed outside the gates. "You don't care about us or the land," they shout. They also complain to their local politicians and, as a result, the city drags its feet rather than issue a building permit. Meanwhile, bad press about Tradescant Rose builds and builds. "Why are they doing this to us?" asks the director.

In another city, the Most Fabulous Art Museum is under pressure to diversify its audience. "Let's create an art van and send it out into the community," suggests the museum's director. He hires a community affairs manager but gives her no staff and only limited resources. She asks senior management for a year to prepare the community for the van; her plan is to visit local religious congregations and community centers and even go door-to-door to get the word out. "I need to develop relationships in the community," she explains. "Right now, people have no connection to the museum." Management's response? "You don't have a year; our grant funding doesn't cover that." After much fanfare, the art van is sent out into the community. No one comes.

These scenarios are based on actual events at two very reputable institutions. I mention them to shed some light on why museums must establish and maintain an ongoing dialogue with their communities. As museum staff work with limited budgets, staff, and resources—often spread too thin and feeling overwhelmed—involving the community sometimes feels like one more thing you just don't have the time to do. But the museum-community relationship is one that must be nurtured if our institutions are to succeed at their mission to serve the public good.

Through its Museums and Community Initiative (M&C), the American Association of Museums strives to support and assist the museum field as it works to strengthen its relationships with its communities. Established in 1998 by AAM's board of directors, M&C was conceived as a broad-based collaborative process, involving a national task force, six community dialogues, and continuing conversations between community leaders and the museum field.

During the M&C dialogues, it soon became clear that while museums are viewed as trusted and respected institutions, many community members also see them as elitist and aloof. Holding a community dialogue can be a powerful first step in changing the dynamics of the museum-community relationship. If we really listen to the voices in our communities, we'll discover innovative and exciting ways of approaching our public activities. Ongoing conversations also will encourage us to evaluate our current efforts to engage the community. As one M&C dialogue participant said, "I thought our institution was deeply engaged with its community until I [was] asked to come up with a significant community participant list for the event. All I could think of were the usual suspects. That's when it hit home that there was still a great deal of work to be done."

Let me emphasize that holding a dialogue is only one step in the process. As noted in *Mastering Civic Engagement: A Challenge to Museums* (MCE), the companion publication to this toolkit, becoming a more civically engaged and community-conscious museum requires an internal inquiry in addition to the external one represented by the dialogues. The internal inquiry should be a sincere exploration—involving staff, board, and volunteers—of such areas as individual and institutional attitudes; organizational practices; issues of ownership, access, and trust; and museum-community relationships. (For more information about conducting an internal inquiry, see pages 9 to 20 of MCE.) Preferably, this work should be undertaken before, or at least at the same time, the museum begins its efforts to become more involved in the community. And it must be institution-wide so that each staff member, volunteer, and board member has a clear understanding about the museum's mission, objectives, and goals for its relationship with its community. Otherwise you might hear a comment similar to this one voiced by a community participant at an M&C dialogue: "[At X] Museum, it depends on what department you are dealing with. Some [staff] get it; some don't."

During the dialogues, many community participants who had worked with museums in the past expressed frustration with and a mistrust of their local museums. Said one participant: "The museum only comes to me when they need to trot me [around] to funders to demonstrate how diverse they are. When this happens, I am required to support their agenda. It's not a real partnership." As described in *Museums in the Life of a City: Strategies for Community Partnerships*, partnerships with the community require a strong commitment from the museum, in terms of leadership, staff time, resources, attitude, patience, flexibility, etc. Without that commitment, a museum's overtures to the community are likely to fail.

Making the museum's processes, decision-making, and actions open, available, and understandable to the public is not just a smart survival tactic, it is the right thing do. Most of us became museum professionals because we wanted to make a difference in the world. Here is our chance to do so, and we can't let the fact that we have "too much other work" stand in our way.

Kim Igoe is project director, Museums & Community, and vice president, policy & programs, AAM

Giving Voice:
A Role for Museums in Civic Dialogue

by Barbara Schaffer Bacon, Pam Korza, and Patricia E. Williams

GIVING VOICE:
A ROLE FOR MUSEUMS IN CIVIC DIALOGUE

By Barbara Schaffer Bacon, Pam Korza, and Patricia E. Williams

As David Thelen wrote in "Learning Community: Creating the Civic Museum" (Museum News, May/June 2001), "We are living at a time when museums and other meaning-making institutions of popular education and culture are reconsidering their civic mission and practices, the places they seek, the ways they engage new partners and audiences, and, therefore, their priorities. Many believe that the health of these institutions depends on becoming more civically engaged with a range of communities."

But how can museums achieve this civic mission? As Thelen states, museums are not the only organizations working to reinvent themselves as civically engaged institutions, and there is much that we can learn from our colleagues.

Launched in 1999 by Americans for the Arts, the Animating Democracy Initiative—like AAM's Museums & Community Initiative—encourages cultural organizations to explore their civic role. This essay provides a broader sense of the spectrum of civic engagement available to museums— from incorporating a dialogue component into exhibit programming to an institutional exploration of a museum's civic mission and goals. While the examples discussed below focus on programming, ADI has come to recognize that program-based dialogue is most successful when it is part of a museum-wide effort to become a civic institution.

There is a growing movement to reinvigorate civic dialogue as a vital dimension of a healthy democracy, based on the premise that a democracy is animated by an informed public engaged in the issues affecting their daily lives. Civic dialogue plays an essential role in this process, giving voice to multiple perspectives and enabling people to develop more multifaceted, humane, and realistic views of complex issues and of each other. Yet opportunities for civic dialogue in this country have diminished in recent years, due mainly to polarization of opinion along ideological, racial, gender, and class lines; social structures that separate rich from poor and majorities from minorities; a sense of individual disempowerment; and the over-whelming nature of many of society's problems. Perhaps most fundamentally, the fact that modern problems usually affect different people in different ways often places them outside of the traditional civic organization, labor unions, and political parties that organized civic discourse in the past.

Through its Animating Democracy Initiative, Americans for the Arts aims to explore and enhance the potential of the arts and humanities to illuminate civic experience and to strengthen the role or arts and cultural institutions in civic discourse. The Animating Democracy Lab, a component of the initiative, supports 32 civic dialogue projects at several cultural institutions, including four museums. Individually and collectively, these diverse projects are advancing knowledge about the philosophical, practical, and social dimensions of arts-based civic dialogue. All over the country, museums and other cultural organizations are using arts and humanities resources to advance civic dialogue.

With the thoughtful and imaginative use of basic collection, preservation, exhibition, and education functions, museums can expand the debate on important contemporary issues by providing forums for civic dialogue. Through intentional and focused public discussions of the civic issues, policies, and decisions that affect people's lives, museums can expand opportunity for democratic participation by encouraging broader, more diverse publics to give voice to the critical issues of our time.

What Is Civic Dialogue?

The Study Circles Resource Center, a national organization devoted to community-wide dialogue on a range of contemporary issues, defines dia-logue as a purposeful process in which two or more parties with differing viewpoints work toward common understanding in an open-ended, (usually) face-to-face format. In *The Magic of Dialogue*, sociologist Daniel Yankelovich cites the characteristics that make dialogue so vital in a democracy. "Dialogue is distinguished from simple discussion and adversarial debate in several important ways," he writes:

> Dialogue encourages participants to *suspend judgment* and allow assumptions and preconceptions to be brought out into the open, in order to foster under-standing and break down obstacles. It attempts to create *equality* among participants, seeking ways to even out inequalities in levels of information about the issue, experience in public forums, and real or perceived positions of power or authority. It encourages *empathy* by inviting *multiple perspectives* to the table and supporting their expression, thus facilitating a greater understanding of others' viewpoints. Through these and other means, it seeks to build a climate of trust and safety, without which genuine dialogue cannot occur.

Civic dialogue brings these characteristics into the public realm.

What Assets Does a Museum Have to Offer?

- *Individual objects or collection-based and special exhibitions* can provide a focal point for civic dialogue. "Gene(sis): Contemporary Art Explores Human Genomics," a 2002 exhibition at the University of Washington's Henry Art Gallery in Seattle, featured the work of artists responding to recent developments in the science of human genomics. As curators developed the exhibition, scientists worldwide were completing the map of the human genome. With that and Seattle's own vigorous biogenetic industry and research activity as context, the Henry's curators saw the exhibition as a prime opportunity to focus public attention on and deepen understanding of the social, ethical, and economic implications of bio-genetics. Media coverage and visitor feedback suggest that the exhibition, public dialogue programs, and linked activities succeeded in raising con-sciousness and stimulating thought and discussion.

- *Educational guides and activities* can help participants find points of departure for inquiry and dialogue. The Henry—in conjunction with a dialogue advisor and educators from several local schools, and drawing on dialogues with members of the scientific community—developed an exceptional curriculum guide for teachers. The guide introduced concepts of dialogue and civic dialogue and provided issue-based resources teachers could use to prepare students for their visit. The Henry also adapted its Visual Thinking Strategies approach to gallery education, to move visitors from an exploration of the art to a discussion of genomics issues.

- *Complementary exhibitions* may offer a contemporary, historic, or global context, as well as contrasts and comparisons that can increase information and understanding around an issue. In 1997, staff at the Wadsworth Athenaeum, Hartford, Conn.—recognizing that the city's history included both the gun-manufacturing legacy of the Colt family and the escalating gun violence of recent years—asked artist Brad McCallum to help them illuminate the seriousness of the issue. McCallum created 228 custom-designed, symbolic manhole covers from tons of confiscated guns and an audio installation capturing stories of Hartford citizens affected by gun violence, the latter developed through interviews and dialogue. *The Manhole Cover Project* was exhibited outside the museum (and, later, the manhole covers were installed in the streets of the city). Inside, the Wadsworth mounted an exhibition from its collection of the Colt family's art treasures. The joint exhibition combined a historic reference and contemporary art to focus on a pressing current issue.

- *Museum galleries, meeting rooms, education facilities, and auditoria* are appropriate physical spaces for hosting dialogues, and may offer the right contextual spaces as well. In spring 2002, the Jewish Museum, New York, took a great risk with its own community when it presented "Mirroring Evil: Nazi Imagery/Recent Art," a controversial exhibition that shifted focus from victims to perpetrators. Asking, "Who can speak for the Holocaust?" the exhibition tread morally ambiguous ground. Could another museum have mounted the exhibition and facilitated difficult dialogues within the Jewish community on this topic? Museum leaders believed that the institution's venerated position within the Jewish community as well as its sensitivity to the issue and its stakeholders meant it could undertake this controversial exhibition responsibly.

- *Professional expertise of staff* in areas of research, conservation, education, curation, promotion, or management may be of great benefit to other efforts in a community whose goal is civic dialogue. The Lower East Side Tenement Museum, New York, is lending its organizing and coalition-building skills, as well as its knowledge of historic sites of conscience, to the restoration of 19th-century slave galleries located in the nearby St. Augustine's Episcopal Church. The museum is helping to develop training for community preservationists affiliated with the church and other ethnic, social, and religious institutions, which will use the slave galleries as a symbolic space for dialogue about persistent issues of marginalization in the neighborhood. Leaders in neighborhood organizations—including the Trust in God Baptist Church, Eldridge Street Project, United Neighborhood Houses, Good Ol' Lower East Side, as well as the museum and the church's Slave Galleries Committee—have been involved intensively in the project and also received training in facilitating dialogue. Many other community organizations—such as the Boys Club, synagogues, libraries, schools, and human service organizations—have participated in dialogues convened by these community preservationists.

One Story: An Exhibit Inspires a Dialogue on Race

The arts and humanities can help reinvigorate dialogues that have reached an impasse, mobilize diverse players, or simply encourage people to take up a difficult issue. Talking about contentious themes and different people's points of view can help reveal the assumptions of an individual or community and open a previously closed topic to fruitful discourse. Even provocative or controversial shows can lead to thoughtfully planned dialogues on civic issues that help communities in vital and valuable ways.

For example, Pittsburgh's Andy Warhol Museum used a dialogue approach to engage community partners in the development of an exhibition and to advance dialogue on a key civic issue. Through its 2001 presentation of "Without Sanctuary: Lynching Photography in America"—an exhibition of horrific images showing men and women being lynched—the museum aimed to create a platform for conversations about the city's racial conflicts. With tensions running high after a spate of racially motivated killings, museum staff listened closely to community voices to create an environment in which people would feel safe engaging and discussing the disturbing photographs. They engaged a community advisory group and numerous religious and civic organizations to help plan the exhibit, provide extensive background material, and create discussion opportunities. They also conferred with colleagues at the New-York Historical Society, which had previously shown the exhibition.

The museum engaged stakeholders with connections to African-American communities, as well as schools, diverse community organizations, and a broad cross-section of individual community, religious, business, and political leaders. Staff tried to include organizations concerned with improving race relations in the planning and co-sponsoring of events, and held several meetings to talk about "Without Sanctuary," listening to concerns and acting on advice. With a consciousness enabled through the Warhol's partnership with the YWCA Center for Race Relations, stakeholders began to use the principles and practices of dialogue to navigate their differences and ideas.

The museum's main gallery provided a detailed context for the subject of lynching and its history—featuring the "Without Sanctuary" photographs, historical artifacts, and contemporary artwork—and also provided spaces for written and videotaped visitor comments. After viewing the exhibition, visitors were encouraged to move to a second gallery and join one of the daily dialogues. (In this room, anti-lynching quotes covered the walls, and books on lynching and related subjects, as well as information on organizations, groups, and activities for "next steps," also were available.) The dialogues were co-led by the museum's artist/educators (practicing artists with experience in education and community-based art practice) and community facilitators from the Pittsburgh branch of the National Association for the Advancement of Colored People (NAACP), the National Conference for Community and Justice (NCCJ), the Urban League of Pittsburgh, and the YWCA Center for Race Relations, among others.

More than 31,000 people saw the exhibition, and approximately 1,000 engaged in the dialogue sessions. According to museum staff, wonderful relationships and conversations developed among the participants and among the artist/educators and community facilitators, which greatly enhanced the relationship between the museum and its community. "Whether they were considering issues of race in America and their role in it for the very first time, or were voicing opinions they had held and secretly thought for years and had never expressed," says artist/educator Sarah Williams, "almost everyone who came to the school/public dialogues came away exposed to new thinking."

The activity surrounding the exhibition also drew local media attention, which, in turn, prompted further public discourse. The exhibition thus provoked multiple and intersecting ripples of dialogue among visitors to the exhibition, between the museum and its partners, within the large community planning committee, and in the institution itself, among the staff, board, and artist-educators.

"From an internal perspective, the cross-departmental and institution-wide collaboration and joint leadership enabled the project to be fully embraced by the entire museum, which in turn enhanced our position with our communities," says Jessica Arcand, curator of education and co-director of the "Without Sanctuary" project. "From an external perspective, the collaboration was successful because of the critical personal relationships [we developed] but also because we were able to listen, hear and value the diverse points of view we heard as much as our own."

Best Practices for Civic Dialogue

When a museum mounts an exhibition as part of a civic dialogue strategy, curatorial and interpretive considerations must be balanced against the goals of the dialogue. To be successful, a dialogue should include not only public forums with opportunities for exchange, but also the intentional inclusion and active participation of people with a stake in the issue, as informants or even collaborators in the curatorial process. Though such collaboration may be perceived as infringing on curatorial autonomy and authority, for many curators, the choice to venture into civic terrain yields powerful results—from reconsideration of familiar or known works to fresh approaches to form, content, and process in the creation of exhibitions. Such innovations enhance an audience's experience and provide a rich basis for considering contemporary issues. For curators at the Andy Warhol Museum, the intersection of the gallery and the people offered fertile ground for programmatic innovation.

Conventional elements of a museum's educational and outreach activity can be adapted to promote dialogue about an exhibit's subject matter and to shift from solely disseminating information to encouraging purposeful exchange around the civic issue. Fully integrating dialogue opportunities into an exhibition requires internal and external collaboration. Communication and coordination among education and curatorial staff is critical. Every one in the museum, from trustees to security guards, should have an understanding of exhibition goals and program plans.

Whether seeking to engage the public in self-assessment through dialogue or to employ its art or humanities collections and resources as catalysts for civic dialogue, museums should be aware of several key practices that are crucial for success.

- *Active involvement of stakeholders* in planning can be critical to framing stimulating and relevant questions, attracting desired participants, sustaining interest, or fulfilling a call for action.

- *Frequent, varied, and sustained approaches* to dialogue can allow adequate focus, involve people in a variety of ways to accommodate differences, and, over the long term, contribute significantly to establishing the museum as a valuable convener of civic dialogue.

- *Effective facilitation* is essential to the successful conduct of public dialogues. Sensitive, knowledgeable facilitators can foster a sense of trust, respect, and safety; encourage participation; make perceptive connections between the exhibit and the issue; and help participants link personal experiences to universal themes or current controversies.

- A *"safe" space* must be created so participants feel comfortable enough to engage in difficult exchanges. It must be neutral so that each participant will trust that his perspective will be heard and respected. Creating a safe environment is often a fundamental challenge for some institutions that have been seen as elitist, exclusionary, or simply irrelevant to the life of the community. But creating such a space in a place previously considered "off limits" or dismissed altogether could be one of the most salutary benefits of a successful dialogue.

Museums should consider how their contributions might have the most meaningful impact. What conversations are already happening? Which approaches are seen as constructive or destructive? How is the media covering the issue? Have there been previous attempts to have a dialogue? What was useful; what wasn't? What healed; what divided? What purpose would a dialogue serve and how could the institution support that purpose? Which community partners can help the museum create trust, a safe or equitable space, and authentic connection with various constituents?

Museums also should think about the goals of civic dialogue. What difference does the institution hope to make? Is a dialogue enough? Action or change may indeed be a desirable outgrowth of a dialogue, but a museum-based civic dialogue can contribute to the community in a number of ways. If the public takes notice of an issue; if people are talking, listening, and new voices and perspectives are being heard; if the stakeholders are finally at the table together in a respectful, equitable environment—these are all important indicators of success.

For a museum to expand its vision and facilitate civic engagement it must re-examine long-held perceptions from many perspectives. Dialogue methodology, as described in *Mastering Civic Engagement: A Challenge to Museums* and further detailed in this toolkit, can be a dynamic tool for soliciting and talking about those perceptions and perspectives and further defining the museum's potential civic roles. Because museums are important community institutions, such dialogues have an intrinsically civic dimension and value. *New York Times* critic Michael Kimmelman has observed that the purview of museums now extends well beyond objects to ideas. Museums, he wrote in "Museums in a Quandary" (Aug. 26, 2001), are "storehouses of collective values and diverse histories, places where increasingly we seem to want to spend our free time and thrash out big issues." As the Warhol and other institutions have discovered, museums can be invaluable partners in efforts to spark civic interest and animate dialogue about important issues in their own communities and beyond.

Barbara Schaffer Bacon and Pam Korza direct the Animating Democracy Initiative for Americans for the Arts in Washington, D.C. Patricia E. Williams, vice president and COO at Americans for the Arts, is the former vice president, policy and programs, AAM, and was the first project director of the Museums & Community Initiative.

Americans for the Arts is the nation's leading nonprofit organization for advancing the arts in America, dedicated to creating opportunities for every American to participate in and appreciate all forms of the arts. The Animating Democracy Initiative (ADI) is a project of Americans for the Arts Institute for Community Development and the Arts and is made possible with support from The Ford Foundation.

Designing a Community Dialogue

DESIGNING A COMMUNITY DIALOGUE

. . . .

Community dialogues were a central part of Museums & Community (M&C) —AAM's national initiative to explore how museums can build dynamic relationships with their communities. In 2000 and 2001, dialogues were held in Providence; Tampa; Los Angeles; Detroit; Wichita; and Bellingham, Wash.— a representative cross-section of the many communities in which museums are located. Each community illustrated a different set of challenges to practicing civic engagement and exploring how museums could be active participants in the process.

The dialogues were richly rewarding, many times in unexpected ways. They produced a wealth of insights that might not have been uncovered in any other setting or using any other process. Although the M&C Project Team developed a common framework for the dialogues, each one reflected its own community and the variety of people and perspectives that came together.

At the end of the dialogues, AAM felt there was a residual value in what we had learned—both about gathering community members and museums for a productive conversation, and about encouraging other museums to organize similar events focused on building community connections. AAM's process brought together a significant number of museums to help plan and convene the dialogue. A museum interested in organizing a community dialogue might choose to focus only its own particular interests or bring other museums together for the purpose. Such decisions will influence the scale of the final dialogue, from the size and composition of the steering committee to the size of the ultimate gathering to the way the dialogue design is adapted to make it as relevant and useful as possible.

What follows is a short list of things to consider when convening a museum-community dialogue. By sharing what we learned, we hope to help you circumvent a few pitfalls and build a dialogue in which people feel welcome, heard, and rewarded for their efforts.

A A M ' s   G o a l s

What were the goals of the M&C dialogues?

M&C had a specific focus: to discover whether museums could play a significant role in, and redefine their relationships with, their communities, and whether communities could see museums as legitimate and useful partners. Through M&C, AAM sought to bring museums into a broader national conversation about the way people and organizations connect in contemporary society. AAM's formal goals were to:

- engage broad cross-sections of the community in a dialogue about the role of museums that would have a long-lasting value to the various cities

- allow a large number of people—with deep experience about the community but an unknown level of experience about museums—to have a good conversation with their museum counterparts

- invite people to provide useful, insightful information about the role of the museum in the community

- encourage museums and communities to develop ongoing relationships with each other

Likewise, a museum convening its own dialogue—particularly one with people who have no formal relationship with and limited knowledge about museums—should develop a clear sense of its goals, purposes, and readiness to take action.

Why were the M&C dialogues unique for AAM?

Building upon AAM's earlier experiences involving the community, these conversations were populated primarily by people who did not work in museums. Their design and format provided AAM with the opportunity to examine how communities view and use museums, and see whether communities could imagine museums playing a larger role in building community health and well being. The dialogues also encouraged the museum participants to consider how their institutions might function as civic enterprises and create deep and ongoing relationships among diverse groups.

Which resources aided the planning of the M&C dialogues?

Ideas and theories about how civil societies develop have been fairly rigorously debated in other fields, in this country and abroad. Sociologist Robert Putnam, for example, has conducted extensive research on the development of civil societies. When the dialogues began, he had just published a book about civil societies and social capital called *Bowling Alone: The Collapse and Revival of American Community*, which examines how people connect or disconnect from each other socially and as members of a community.

Francis Fukuyama, best-known for *The End of History*, also wrote *Trust: The Social Virtues and the Creation of Prosperity*. This book examines the extent to which the success of culture, economies, and democracies is based on how much people trust and depend on each other to be honest, do good work, and meet their obligations, whether or not there's an immediate reward for their efforts.

Other publications describe international settings where religious, cultural, and ethical traditions are different from those of the United States and consider how certain philosophies or world views impeded the development of strong communities in the 20th century. In addition, the Pew Charitable Trusts and other organizations have undertaken significant projects to measure aspects of social capital. For a list of resources, see page XX.

T h e   P a r t i c i p a n t s

In each community, it was the participants who influenced the tone of the M&C dialogues and determined their success. People who did wonderful work in their communities took the time to talk to each other, to AAM, and to museum staff and trustees about their experiences with museums. Many participants had hands-on roles in their communities—working, for example, with low-income housing, new immigrant populations, and law enforcement, rather than at the public policy level. In each city, the staffs of several types of museums were inspired not only by their community colleagues but by each other as well. Together, participants from museums and communities speculated about how they might join together to make communities healthier, safer, and better places to live.

Who should come to a community dialogue?

A community dialogue should include a broad and diverse cross-section of community stakeholders, including representatives from community organizations, social-service providers, faith-based organizations, educational institutions, and the media. Other participants might include representatives from state and local government, architecture and urban planning, technology, philanthropy, business, and museums. (For a list of the groups AAM targeted, see "Potential Participants.") The invitees should have one thing in common: they should all be involved in the day-to-day business of building community, serving communities, and/or linking communities and museums, and should expect to represent the community-at large.

The most successful M&C dialogues were those whose participants were responsible on a daily basis for solving problems; making things work, helping people, and managing programs and budgets. Dialogues were less successful when the participants' occupations focused on giving opinions, developing policy, or public advocacy. The success of the dialogues also depended on the participation of the museum leaders in the various communities—executive directors and trustees. A museum's ability to deeply engage with its community requires the support of its leaders. Without their presence and active support, new museum-community connections will not be nurtured, and organizations will find it more difficult to implement change.

Initially, the M&C Project Team thought that it would be difficult to persuade community leaders to attend, but that concern proved to be unwarranted. Community leaders were more than willing to spend a day discussing museums. They were far more interested in our institutions than might have been expected; several said they were flattered to be asked to share their perspective. Museum professionals often showed a greater reluctance to participate, citing a lack of staff, limited resources, and excessive workloads.

How many people should attend the dialogue?

Invite enough individuals to get a diverse cross-section of community life, but not so many people that it is difficult to have a useful and satisfying conversation. That might mean as few as 25 or as many as 60 people. The tighter the group, the better the dialogue, and participants will be better able to imagine themselves collaborating on an ongoing basis. With approximately 110 attendees at each M&C dialogue, AAM did succeed in engaging a large number of individuals. However, it was difficult to coordinate the event and manage an engaging dialogue with so many people.

Should participants receive any preparatory materials?

Enhance the conversation by encouraging participants to think about museums and community in the days and weeks before the dialogue takes place. For example, the M&C Project team sent participants a copy of "Points of View: A Pre-Meeting Exercise" (see page 41), asking them to complete the exercise and return it to AAM approximately two weeks before the event. "Points of View" allowed the team to collect important information about who would take part in the dialogue. Participants were asked:

• to relate a fact about their community, or another community, that might surprise people but also made a powerful statement about museums and community (for example, a participant at the Los Angeles M&C dialogue noted that his city leads the country in the purchase of books; yet this reading public does not attend museum exhibitions at a comparable level)

• to relate a fact about themselves—their current work, their experience, the issues they feel strongly about—that illuminated their personal and professional perspectives on communities and museums

Depending upon whether they were community or museum participants, participants were asked to tell a short story that typified either their museum's engagement with the community or their organization's involvement with museums. Community participants who were not involved with a local museum were asked to suggest ways of making that connection happen.

How can you ensure that participants will speak the same language?

M&C's most successful dialogues employed a panel of speakers, who established the framework and introduced new concepts and vocabulary in a formal way, explaining what was meant by community, civil society, community building, and social capital, etc. That allowed everyone to participate in the dialogue right away. These concepts—which are discussed in detail in *Mastering Civic Engagement: A Challenge to Museums*, this toolkit's companion publication—may be relatively new to first-time dialogue participants; people will need guidance if they are to arrive at a conceptual understanding early enough in the day. If an appropriate speaker is not available, museums may want to provide a glossary or other written material about these ideas to participants before the event. (See also "M&C Dialogue Definitions.")

Do community participants have to be knowledgeable about, or even familiar with, museums?

Community participants should be thoughtful and committed to the community's success, but they don't have to be major consumers of museums or have experience partnering with museums on outreach or community projects. The M&C dialogue design gave all participants the opportunity to talk about how they perceived museums and what they valued about them, and to compare museums to other community institutions, such as libraries, galleries, and other gathering places. A significant part of each dialogue drew on what participants knew best: where their communities came together, where they celebrated, and the kinds of things that drove people apart. The dialogue design emphasized community knowledge over museum knowledge and made it easier for people to delve quickly into the day's agenda.

What challenges might museum staff encounter during a dialogue?

The M&C project explored concepts and ideas that were new to many museum professionals. The underlying question—whether museums can function as civic enterprises—was different from the issues museums usually tackle, for example, increasing "community outreach" or reaching out to "underserved" or "new" audiences. Many museums had not consciously examined their own role as citizens in their communities, and they hadn't thought about how the community might contribute to their institutions.

A smaller challenge lay in getting the museum participants to accept, with patience, the sometimes uninformed ideas and out-of-date opinions that surfaced during the dialogue. In the interest of keeping the dialogues open and speculative, the M&C project team tried to dissuade museum people from pointing out what already was being done, or wouldn't work, or had been tried before. The challenge usually was overcome over the course of the day, due to the thoughtfulness and seriousness of the community participants and also by the number of new people and organizations the museums encountered.

A museum (or group of museums) convening a dialogue should explore some of the basic ideas about community engagement before forming a steering committee and sending out invitations. Museum staff attending a community dialogue should be encouraged to see their institutions as elements in the fabric of the community, and understand that museums can legitimately respond to different expectations and needs than they had conceived in the past. At the M&C dialogues, for example, museums began to recognize that they have assets beyond their exhibitions and education programs—including their staffs, buildings, and collections, and their roles as safe spaces and community-gathering places. (For a discussion of museum assets, see pages 35-36 of *Mastering Civic Engagement*.)

Civic engagement is not about audience development, reaching out to underserved audiences, or building programs that serve one specific group. Instead, it is about involving the museum in the life of its community. For many museum staffers, the dialogue might provide a first opportunity to talk with a representative from a nonprofit housing corporation, a bank officer who loans money for community development, or someone from a group that shelters the homeless. These and other community representatives will encourage museums to see the opportunities for collaboration, view their physical and human assets as part of the cityscape, and play a role in addressing or solving community problems.

The Steering Committee

To engage a new set of partners, a museum (or group of museums) should convene a committee that can lead the institution to the diverse places in its community. AAM organized steering committees, which determined the content, whom to invite, and where to hold the dialogues. Without these committees, the dialogues would not have been genuine discussions about the participating communities. The participants the committees chose influenced the quality of the dialogue and determined whether it would have an impact on the community.

What is the role of the steering committee?

In addition to providing support and leadership for the event, the steering committee ensures that the dialogue reflects the life of the community. The museum will furnish the framework for the dialogue, and the steering committee will influence the content. Committee members help identify important community issues that can be woven into the dialogue design. That process is essential for ensuring that the dialogue is not museum-driven but an open and honest discussion, among a broad range of local stakeholders, about how the museum can explore a civic mission and increase its value and relevance to its communities.

Committee members also can help the museum by providing the names and addresses of potential participants; making follow-up calls (if necessary) to encourage invitees to attend; and, of course, attending the dialogue.

The committee chair (or co-chairs) should sign the invitation letter sent to potential participants, which should explain the purpose of the dialogue clearly.

Who should sit on the steering committee?

The steering committee should reflect the scope and diversity of the museum's community. For example, the M&C steering committees were 65 percent community and 35 percent museum, thus allowing a broad but proportionate group of museum leaders to participate in the process. It is preferable, though not absolutely necessary, that community leaders serving on the steering committee have some previous experience working with their local museums; that will enable them to contribute to the process immediately. Since the goal of the dialogue is to engage the broadest cross-section of the community, look for well-connected individuals who wear many hats and who may not have been involved with the museum in the past. Steering committee members should be expected to present not only their personal perspectives but also those of their constituents.

The Logistics

The schedule, the facility, the room, and the guidance given to the facilitator —these factors all play a role in determining the success of a dialogue.

How do you choose the site for a dialogue?

The dialogue's location is important, both symbolically and practically. Is the site centrally located? Is it a welcoming place? (A formal, stuffy venue might send the wrong message.) Does it offer free parking? Is it in a neutral space—a city library, academic institution, or community center—rather than in the museum itself? (The offices of a local funder, for example, might attract many people to the event, but discourage honest, open discourse.)

Think, too, about the room itself, which should comfortably accommodate the attendees and be ADA compliant. (For more information about ADA compliance, see *Everyone's Welcome: The Americans with Disabilities Act and Museums*, AAM, 1995.) The room should be well lit and place the facilitator in full view of all participants. It should be insulated from outside noise or have the audio equipment (and the staff to operate it) that will allow everyone to hear. It also should be close to phones and restrooms.

What is the best way to set up the room?

Round tables are critical for a successful dialogue. They encourage introductions and make small-group discussions possible. Moving participants around at different points in the day allows them to meet more people than they might if the room were configured differently. It also lets participants move away from those whose voices are too strong or insistent and gives them a chance to recharge their batteries by working with different groups. The M&C dialogues incorporated careful seating plans that created balance and variety throughout the day.

Can the schedule influence the content of the dialogue?

The M&C dialogues required a framework that would allow for a coherent, sustained conversation over several hours. In addition, the topics covered in the dialogue design had to be general enough to engage a broad cross-section of participants. Neither of these considerations, however, may apply to a museum convening its own set of dialogues. A museum might plan a shorter conversation and/or choose more specific topics, appropriate to its needs.

AAM's first dialogue took place over a day and half, and included a reception at a museum at the end of the first day. While there was merit to participants getting acquainted at a social event, trying to sustain the conversation, and even keep people in the room, for more than a day was difficult. As a result, each subsequent dialogue took place during a single day.

What is the facilitator's role?

A good facilitator should move participants effortlessly through the rhythms of the dialogue. Far more than anyone, she sets the tone for the day. Her style should be neutral, supportive, and designed to elicit the most out of participants. As *New Visions: Tools for Change in Museums* states, while the facilitator may define the parameters for the dialogue process, she should not influence the group's conclusions. Participants may become angry or disillusioned if they feel they are being talked down to or lectured by the facilitator.

Specifically, the facilitator should perform the following functions:

- ensure that participants have time at the start to become comfortable with the room, relax, and begin to process their thoughts
- control the flow and guide the agenda
- ensure that everyone has a chance to participate equally

- maintain a climate in which everyone feels comfortable and willing to contribute

- manage conflict

- ask clarifying questions and solicit feedback

- ensure that there is general acceptance of the conclusions reached by the group

- ensure that there is a post-dialogue "cool-down" that includes evaluation of the progress participants have made during the course of the day and of the dialogue itself, planning of future dates and activities, clarification of responsibilities, and timetables for action plans.

At the start of each M&C dialogue, the facilitator talked about the best ways to have an effective dialogue. She asked participants to pay close attention, tell the truth, be open to a variety of outcomes, and help the group arrive at a shared understanding about museums and community.

What is the best way to record people's comments?

Recording people's comments on flip charts is a critical part of the process. The visual affirmation allows participants to know their ideas have been captured for the entire group to see. It also is an extremely useful tool when small-group discussions are reported to the larger group. At the M&C dialogues, participants were encouraged to designate a recorder to capture each small group's thinking on a flip chart. At one dialogue where these instructions were not emphasized, it became clear that when people couldn't see their ideas in front of them, they became disorganized and frustrated.

How can you ensure that every participant's voice is heard?

It is important to honor the efforts of the participants, who will put a great deal of work into the dialogue. However, it isn't feasible to listen to several groups of people describe what may be very similar work products. At the M&C dialogues, the facilitator asked two or three groups to report on their projects in full, and others to talk about certain aspects of the assignment or make specific comments about their colleagues' reports. That allowed all participants to feel that they had a voice in the conversation.

As stated in New Visions, *dialogue is more about consensus building or problem solving than about conversing. It is intentional and purposeful rather than casual and inconsequential. Dialogue is a fundamental tool that allows participants to think together and learn from one another. New Visions outlines the following conditions as crucial to a dialogue's success: inclusion of the stakeholders; openness and honesty; participation; mutual respect (of participants and facilitator); a tolerance of ambiguity (on behalf of the participants and organizers); and identification and suspension of assumptions.*

Is it possible for a large group of people to connect with each other?

With the large number of participants at the M&C dialogues, there wasn't time for people to introduce themselves formally to everyone in the room. The issue of introductions in any group of more than a dozen is always a challenge. While introductions are essential and a hallmark of polite behavior, they can absorb a lot of valuable time and create a serious loss of momentum.

On the other hand, building introductions in the community was one of the project's goals. AAM found that placing round tables around the meeting room created more opportunities for people to meet each other. In addition, when people spoke to the larger group for the first time, the facilitator asked them to introduce themselves; that gave everyone a sense of who was in the room—from names and faces to institutional affiliations and roles in the community.

The design of the dialogue also facilitated more personal interactions. The format called for participants to alternate between large- and small-group discussions (centered at the tables at which they were seated). Individuals also were asked "to play musical chairs" (i.e., move to a different table) at least twice during the day, and introduce themselves to a new set of table mates. The seating assignments throughout the day were planned carefully to maintain a balance between museum participants and those from the community. The goal was to encourage participants to meet as many people as possible.

With such a diverse group, is it possible to focus a dialogue on the museum-community relationship?

The M&C dialogue design was constructed in a way that encouraged active participation among the attendees. First, to begin the day and ground the conversation, participants were asked to talk about their communities, where people come together and where they separate. During the dialogues, the separations mentioned were usually geographic, economic, or racial. But when people talked about coming together, a fascinating array of obvious and not-so-obvious places were mentioned: Fourth of July celebrations, coffee shops, bookstores, soccer fields, schools, Wal-Mart. By the Los Angeles dialogue, AAM had introduced the idea of "bridging social capital" to describe the places and events in a community that encourage people to overcome the conventional circumstances that separate them from each other, just the way a bridge connects one place to another. The dialogue design then asked people to talk about how they perceive museums and how they value them, personally and as community institutions.

These two sets of questions were addressed to the entire group at the beginning of the dialogue. Participants found them easy to respond to, and they established a useful frame of reference for the rest of the day. They also helped to establish who was in the room, enabled everyone to hear a variety of voices, and encouraged enough participation to make everyone feel comfortable.

It then was possible to ask people to discuss more complicated questions about how a museum might become involved in the life of its community, and generate among the participants a critical level of engagement and a willingness to express their views. Topics for discussion included the museum's potential for solving a problem not usually associated with its mission or agenda; the museum as a neutral but engaged place for exploring community conflict; the museum taking on an activist role, etc.

The discussion culminated in an exercise that asked participants to design a museum whose mission is to build social capital in a community. During the M&C dialogues, small-group discussions on the topics mentioned above led to intriguing and useful ideas, and were the beginnings of extended conversations about future collaborations.

What if the conversation gets heated?

Community dialogues often focus on such potentially divisive topics as racism and economic inequalities, which sometimes can lead to an intense debate. However, a heated conversation can demonstrate that participants are making an effort to discuss difficult issues and are being honest and open—all positive things. AAM's approach was to signal at the beginning of each dialogue, when the rules for engagement were explained, that it was okay to have strong feelings, but that individuals should remain respectful during the debate and try to consider other points of view. The facilitator only intervened if participants got too far off track.

How might people's ideas and perceptions change by the end of the dialogue?

By the end of each M&C dialogue, community representatives said that they saw museums as much more interesting places than they had in the past and could imagine working with museums as serious partners in their own work. Museum staff were able to see their institutional assets in a different light, based on the comments from the community. Participants began designing museums that were open and accessible to all, where the community could see itself in the programming. Whether they were institutions on wheels or located in areas with good parking, the ideal museums that people envisioned were available, recognizable, and accessible. The conclusion of each dialogue included a short conversation, led by the steering committee chairs, that solicited ideas about how to continue the dialogue.

Your Museums & Community Dialogue

Should my museum plan a dialogue following M&C's exact model?

As noted at various points in this section, not necessarily. AAM had to employ a framework that was adaptable to the needs of six different communities, could be used to track national trends, and compressed a lot of conversation into a single day, in a way that made people feel that they'd been involved in a meaningful endeavor.

A museum could organize a highly effective dialogue in a number of different ways. For example, it might organize dialogues on various topics once a month for a six-month period or hold one specific dialogue over a longer period of time. As noted earlier, several publications explain how to build the level of engagement, trust, and goodwill that a group needs to have a good conversation; those resources were factored into M&C's dialogues and would be helpful to any museum designing its own. (See also "Resources.")

What should my museum consider before it designs its own community dialogue?

A community dialogue is an ongoing and inclusive process, during which a museum and its community work together for the betterment of both. The issues explored should have real meaning in the community (e.g., a significant high-school drop-out rate). Once a group of people have been brought together and involved in a lively and thought-provoking dialogue, the process should be collaborative and lead to a long-term change that benefits the community. The group may decide to meet two, three, four, or more times, or on an as needed basis, and the museum should be prepared for that as it begins to plan the event. Ideally, the conversation will occur over a certain period of time, with the same people coming together on a regular basis to talk about issues that will change and mature over time.

There is no one model for holding a community dialogue. Each dialogue should be unique and reflect the specific issues that pertain to the community and its museums.

My institution tried to bring community members to the museum for a discussion and failed. How might we succeed?

People won't attend a dialogue that seems to be organized according to the museum's terms and conditions and at the museum's convenience. When AAM began to organize the M&C dialogues, we sought co-hosts and used a steering committee to build ownership and a measure of control. We were sensitive to the community's calendar and in one case delayed a dialogue to allow the museums to focus on a ballot referendum that required their full attention. We did everything we could to make people feel welcome—from the invitation and the follow-up calls to making sure that people were fed and comfortable at the event. The dialogues allowed several museum leaders to connect with new potential partners and colleagues in ways that could only benefit their institutions, and these opportunities for collaboration often were enhanced when meetings were held in the community—at a university, hotel, or conference center—rather than at the museum.

How does a holding a community dialogue relate to the internal inquiry outlined in *Mastering Civic Engagement: A Challenge to Museums*?

Holding a community dialogue is just one piece of a much larger examination that must take place within museums if they are to master civic engagement. As outlined in *Mastering Civic Engagement*, a museum can begin this transformative process by asking a set of questions about its vision of the museum and the values of the people who work there. While each institution should shape its own individual inquiry—based on its mission and goals—museums might consider the following questions:

Attitudes

- What is the civic purpose of our museum?
- What are our questions, concerns, and conflicts surrounding civic engagement?
- What internal and external perceptions shape our museum's civic engagement?
- Is there internal resistance to civic engagement?
- What behavior—institutional and individual—promotes civic-minded values?
- What behavior stands in the way?

Practice

- Can the governing board legitimately claim to represent the community, and would the community agree?
- Does the museum engage in exclusive practices in any of its operations, including hiring, contracting, and purchasing?
- How should the qualifications of those who work in our museum change?
- Should trustees and museum professionals understand community dynamics as a prerequisite for board service and for employment?
- Should museum professionals view themselves as citizens first and museum staff second?
- What can our museum do to encourage staff to be engaged with the community?
- Do we have the capacity to stimulate systemic change, both within our museum and in the community?

Ownership, Access, and Trust

- Whose viewpoints and voices shape the museum's purpose and programs?
- What is the balance between a museum's authority and the community's desire to develop some aspect of the stories told through exhibitions?
- Does shared authority imply that the museum no longer controls meanings and interpretations?

- Can we think of ourselves as collections of community assets? What are those assets?

- Can we invite the community to help identify assets? Can we work with the community to make best use of those assets?

Relationships

- What are our motivations for relationships in the community?

- What are our skills at developing programmatic relationships?

- What are our skills at developing organization-to-organization relationships?

- If our skills are limited, how will we improve them?

These are just some of the areas you may decide to explore with your internal stakeholders, i.e., your board, staff, and volunteers. The answers to such an internal inquiry will guide the nature and goals of the museum's ongoing dialogue with its community. Begin this process as early as you can; your internal stakeholders will be more likely to develop a shared understanding of what the museum is about, what it stands for, and what its role in the community should be.

Civic engagement is not easy or instantaneous; it is not a one-shot deal. An institution that is civically engaged is committed to being truly inclusive—not just some departments or when it's convenient, but the entire museum, all the time.

Potential Participants

POTENTIAL PARTICIPANTS

. . . .

It is the participants of a community dialogue who determine the level of the conversation that takes place. Generally, a broad group of stakeholders will ensure that more constituencies are represented, more viewpoints are heard, and more connections are made between the museum and its community. Following is a list of categories AAM developed during the planning for the six M&C dialogues. Planning committee members used these categories to assemble lists of invitees in each locale.

- a variety of museum staff (not just directors), with diverse sets of expertise and experience
- academicians/artists/writers/journalists
- futurists
- architects/urban planners
- cultural activists
- individuals with international perspectives
- young people
- museums with rural or suburban constituencies
- arts organizations
- state/local government (e.g., mayors, county commissioners, staff from recreation departments, etc.)
- chambers of commerce
- youth organizations
- parent organizations

- education (higher/middle/elementary)
- historic preservation, conservation, and heritage preservation organizations
- tourism, marketing, and convention & visitor bureaus
- media
- technology companies
- social-service organizations
- neighborhood organizations
- coalition associations
- disability-related organizations
- community-development organizations
- regional-planning organizations
- libraries
- fraternities, sororities, and other service organizations
- United Way and other philanthropic organizations
- foundations (community, corporate)
- healthcare organizations
- law enforcement
- transportation providers
- local businesses, especially small businesses
- international organizations
- faith-based/religious organizations

Points of View: A Pre-Meeting Exercise

POINTS OF VIEW: A PRE-MEETING EXERCISE

. . . .

Once they accepted AAM's invitation to the M&C Dialogue, participants were sent a confirmation letter and a copy of Points of View: A Pre-Meeting Exercise. *This document, returned by participants several weeks before the actual event, allowed AAM and the steering committees to collect important information about the individuals themselves, their personal perspectives, and the organizations they represented. The facilitator also used this information to get everyone on the same page, particularly regarding their views about community. Throughout the day, at appropriate moments, she would read passages aloud to focus the conversation. Sharing people's answers to question 5 proved to be a particularly successful way to get participants' creative juices flowing.*

The (location) Community Dialogue is a structured conversation among people involved in the day-to-day business of building community, serving communities, and linking communities and museums. Our goal is to explore creative alternatives for working together to strengthen communities. The substance of the dialogue will build on the perspectives and experiences that community and museum participants contribute.

We would like to know more about you, your organization, and your point of view. By (date), please respond to the following questions via fax or e-mail (insert contact information here):

1. Name

2. Organization

3. Position title

4. What services do you provide, and for whom?

5. Relate a fact about your community—or another community—that is surprising to most people but makes a powerful statement about museums and communities. (Examples: The average length of time a student spends in the Providence public school system is four years. Pittsburgh has the fastest-growing senior population in the nation.)

6. Relate a fact about yourself—your current work, your experience, the issues you feel strongly about—that illuminates your personal and professional perspective on communities and/or museums.

7. *For community participants:* Tell a short story or describe an experience that typifies your organization's involvement with the museums in your community. What made it successful, or unsuccessful? If you are not involved with museums, what would it take to change that?

8. *For museum participants:* Tell a short story or describe an experience that typifies your museum's engagement with your community. What made it successful, or unsuccessful? List a few examples that reflect your ongoing relationship with the community or the kind of long-term relationship you'd like to see.

Thank you for your response. We look forward to seeing you in (location).

The M&C Dialogue Design

THE M&C DIALOGUE DESIGN

. . . .

Everyone who attended the M&C dialogues received a version of this Dialogue Design as well as a list of participant names and contact information. The facilitator followed this design format, in this sequence, over the course of the day. The dialogue began with a large-group discussion, but broke into more manageable, timed, small-group sessions for answering the exercises. Each small group was asked to identify a discussion leader, who would report to the larger group, and a recorder to write people's comments on a flip chart. Reporting was important, because it allowed AAM to capture the essence of the small-group discussions and the larger group to learn how participants at other tables responded to the exercise.

The design included space for notes by participants. The quotes at the bottom of each page were intended as food for thought as participants worked on the exercises, and echo some of the larger themes that AAM sought to explore through the M&C Initiative. A museum designing its own dialogue might choose to use quotations that relate to its immediate community. We invite you to adapt or photocopy pages 46-63 for use during your own museum-community dialogue. You may prefer to "white out" the page numbers before you make your copies.

Getting Started: Rules for the Dialogue

Think hard.
Be bold.
Speak your mind.
Be willing to challenge and be challenged.
Respect others' opinions and ideas.
What else?

Social capital can be defined simply as a . . . set of informal values or norms shared among members of a group that permits them to cooperate with one another. If members of the group come to expect that others will behave reliably and honestly, then they will come to trust one another. Trust acts like a lubricant that makes any group or organization run more effectively. . . . The norms that produce social capital . . . must substantively include virtues like truth telling, meeting obligations, and reciprocity.

—Francis Fukuyama
"Social Capital," in *Culture Matters: How Values Shape Human Progress.*

Part 1: Vision and Possibility

Intersecting with Museums

- What is your personal relationship with museums? Why might you visit a museum?

- What was the best experience you ever had in a museum? What made it important, exciting, satisfactory? When was this?

• What keeps you away from museums? Do you think you are unique?

• How is a museum different from a library? From a university or art school? From a commercial gallery?

Library patrons feel secure and comfortable as they reach the library entrance with their families and experience something quite different as they approach the museum entrance. As one mother put it, the museum feels too hygienic for her family.
        —From a summary of the Denver Art Museum's project for the Program for Art Museums and Communities, supported by the Pew Charitable Trusts. To access, go to: www.artmusecomm.org/index.html.

Notes

When someone is not happy with something we've done, they won't
write a letter to the museum. They'll just tell someone, who'll tell
someone else, who'll tell someone who works at the museum. The
community gossip tells you if you've done something that is not
successful with the community.

—Charlotte Mano, Program Director,
Wing Luke Asian Museum, Seattle.

Characterizing Community Life

- Think about where you live—what divides the community; what loosens its bonds?

- What limits or restricts community life in your city? Are these issues that other cities share? Are they statewide issues?

- Where in the community do people meet to talk, share ideas, and discuss common concerns?

• Where does the community celebrate?

• What brings people together?

....

*Livability is about restoring lost connections, supporting the diversity
and uniqueness of each community, and strengthening the selection
of amenities that enhance economic competitiveness. In many cases,
it is about creating those qualities where they have not existed—in
rapidly growing edge-cities for instance—or restoring them in places
where they have decayed, as is frequently the case in traditional city
cores.*

—Mark Maves and Stephanie Hodal, "Museums and Livable
Communities," in *Journal of Museum Education* 24, nos. 1 and 2
(1999).

....

Notes

Exercise

Participants should briefly explain to the others at the table the mission and primary constituents of the organizations they serve (i.e., youth and literacy, senior lunch program, etc.).

One person from a non-museum organization should volunteer to have her organization serve as the focal point for the exercise.

Using that organization as the starting point, each table is invited to collaborate with a museum on a program that would benefit your constituents and organization. For a variety of reasons—space, money, time—the program should serve more than a single group or audience. It should be flexible enough and have enough broad appeal to interest at least two other organizations represented at the table.

The program does not have to be conventional but you should be able to imagine it happening in and/or being supported by the museum.

Reminder:
- Start with one organization.
- Build a program that would appeal to or serve at least two others.
- The program should be an imaginable partnership between community organizations and a museum.

....

[We] realized an audience is an audience. You can't [fail to] engage any one group in the audience and still keep [all of your audience]. It's not a minority or a majority issue.
    —Bruce Evans, Former Director, Mint Museum of Art, Charlotte, N.C.

....

Notes

The issue is whether . . . leadership can substitute for disaster in stimulating cultural change.
—Lawrence E. Harrison, foreword to *Culture Matters: How Values Shape Human Progress.*

Exercise

The museum is the site for a luncheon honoring six community leaders for their contributions to the city's renewal. During the event the museum director, who is relatively new to the city, talks with one of the honorees, the executive director of an organization that strives to increase the academic achievement of at-risk students in area high schools. They discuss the challenges that make it hard for local teenagers just to remain in school, never mind succeed there. As the museum director learns more about this issue and the goals of the community organization, he starts to think about how the museum could become involved. Previously the museum's engagement with young people had focused on children in the primary grades and their families. It has had very little contact with teenagers and almost no contact with their families.

The museum director suggests to the community leader that they explore ways to collaborate. Later, at a staff meeting, the director encourages his staff to develop ideas and strategies that would use the museum's assets to address the pressing needs of local high school students.

Outline a possible collaboration between the two organizations. As you discuss the specifics of a collaboration, explore the following questions:

• What assets would each organization bring to a collaboration?

• What limitations would affect either organization's ability to collaborate? Can those limitations be overcome?

• What does success look like—for the organizations involved, for the young people, for the community?

....

Rather than saying, the people in the neighborhood live in the shadow of the museum, we say they live in the light of the museum. . . . We have overshadowed the neighborhood, [but] we would like to think of ourselves as a beacon or a lighthouse . . . something that is safe.
—Francine Kelly, Director of Community Relations,
Indianapolis Children's Museum.

....

Notes

A city-owned museum became a private institution. The campaign to shift financial support from the tax rolls to the community characterized the transition as "going public by going private."

A Museums & Community Toolkit | **55**

Part 3:
Envisioning the Museum at the
Heart of the Community

Exercise

In the morning, we considered the characteristics that unite and separate people in a community. We discussed some of the challenges to museum-community engagement as well as the opportunities that exist for museums seeking to expand their civic role. We now will ask you to imagine a museum that is located at the heart of its community.

A) Imagine that you are part of a planning committee for a new suburban, urban, or rural museum. You believe the museum will help build the social capital of the community in a variety of ways.

- What is the museum's civic purpose? Describe it briefly.

- How does the museum's location contribute to social capital?

- Which of the museum's assets are most supportive of its civic purpose?

B) The museum and a community organization are planning a collaboration at the heart of the new museum. Seeking support, you submit a proposal to a foundation.

- How will the museum's assets be used to contribute to social capital? Outline a collaboration that builds social capital in the community.

- Describe the major elements of the collaboration. Is a particular part of the community or aspect of community life addressed?

- List the ways in which you feel social capital is increased through this collaboration.

....

We joke that our work force, staff, and volunteers are so linked to the community that if we do something wrong, Grandma will scold you and let you know.

—Ron Chew, Director, Wing Luke Asian Museum, Seattle.

....

Notes

We are an institution that tells stories, and you want and need people to help you to do that.
— Irene Hirano, President and Director, Japanese American National Museum, Los Angeles.

Framing Quote

A museum "can be a place to gather and debate community problems and community-based solutions. It can educate citizens in the community's needs. It can train leaders. It can break down isolation, recreate feelings of obligation to one another, reinvigorate civic commitment."

—from "A Vital Community Service,"
(Peoria) Journal Star, *Dec. 8, 1996, p. A4.*

• What themes and ideas emerged over the course of the day?

• What, if any, limitations might affect the museum-community relationship?

• What will you take away from the day?

Notes

Part 4:
Closing Out the Day: Extending the Dialogue

- How do you and your fellow participants plan to continue the dialogue?

All professions are conspiracies against the laity.
        —George Bernard Shaw, *The Doctor's Dilemma*, 1906.

Museums and Community in Action: George Eastman House Connects with Its Neighbors

MUSEUMS AND COMMUNITY IN ACTION: GEORGE EASTMAN HOUSE CONNECTS WITH ITS NEIGHBORS

. . . .

As museums strive to become more civically engaged and community-conscious they can learn from and benefit from their peers in the field. For example, staff at George Eastman House International Museum of Photography and Film in Rochester, N.Y., used a model process to develop their Sept. 11 commemorative events. The way this institution approached the planning process, the mindset of its staff, and their eagerness to engage in dialogues both internally (involving all personnel) and externally (with diverse community partners) are worthy of recognition. This model of civic engagement represents an excellent example of a museum and its community in action. Reflective of its commitment to its local community, George Eastman House received a 2002 Cultural Organization Award for outstanding achievement in the arts from the Arts & Cultural Council for Greater Rochester.

A museum that is engaged with its community is responsive and addresses major issues that affect that community in a timely manner. Such an institution places value on developing and sustaining relationships with community partners so that their combined assets may be shared for the public good. This story shows how one museum helped its neighbors cope with a tragedy and along the way improved and enhanced its relationship with the community.

After the Sept. 11 attacks, George Eastman House International Museum of Photography and Film—like so many museums across the country—sought to help its community cope with the tragic events. Inspired by a patriotic "photo quilt" exhibit posted on the Eastman Kodak Web site and a New York City gallery that solicited photographs from the public for display on its walls, staff quickly organized a show of their own in October 2001. "Ground Zero" presented 38 images from media organizations around the world, particularly the Associated Press and the *New York Times*, focusing on the World Trade Center tragedy. But as staff worked to mount the exhibit, they felt strongly that they could and should do more.

At Eastman House, teams comprised of staff members at all levels meet regularly to identify and discuss a variety of institutional challenges and opportunities. At meetings convened after the tragedy, staff talked about the need to begin planning for Sept. 11, 2002, as early as possible. As noted in *Mastering Civic Engagement: A Challenge to Museums*, a civically engaged museum mines its assets for the betterment of the community. One of Eastman House's assets was its exhibition space. Staff wondered: "Would the community want to help develop a museum exhibit? Could the community benefit from this opportunity?"

"Ground Zero" opened to great praise from the press and public, and program staff began planning in earnest. Was there a way to put the temporary exhibit in a broader context? Should they develop a companion exhibit, perhaps on the war in Afghanistan? How could they incorporate the museum's rich collections? How could they involve the entire museum staff in the process? To further the planning process, Eastman House held a internal town meeting, during which staff viewed a large selection of photographs assembled by the museum's archivist. Each staff member was asked to vote for her top five images and to single out her favorite. Staff chose 130 images from the collection, which later became the basis for an exhibition called "Picturing What Matters: An Offering of Photographs."

But before planning for "Picturing What Matters" could proceed, the museum had to find out what else was happening in the community. In the words of one staff member, "Who [were] we to say what our community need[ed] on Sept. 11?"

O p e n i n g   U p   t h e   D i a l o g u e

In early April 2002, the George Eastman House organized a series of meetings with local stakeholders, including Rochester's mayor, the assistant county executive, and the county historian. Staff soon learned that the county historian had been collecting objects related to the Rochester community's response to Sept. 11—from work gloves schoolchildren decorated for volunteers at Ground Zero to booties for the dogs used in rescue and recovery missions. The museum and the historian agreed to collaborate; sharing their resources would allow the county to expand its archives and give the museum better access to items for display.

The conversations also gave Eastman House an early opportunity to participate in the community's plans for the first anniversary of Sept. 11. Mayor William A. Johnson said that he would eagerly support the museum's efforts, and the museum and the city kept talking throughout May and June. Those discussions allowed the museum to identify the stakeholders critical to the community dialogue. "It's just like networking for a job," says Eliza Benington Kozlowski, Eastman's director of communications and visitor services. "Now, who else do you suggest we talk to? Months later, we are still learning about people [who should] be involved."

The museum's potential partners in the Sept. 11, 2002, planning efforts included the police and sheriff's departments, the Rochester chapter of the American Red Cross, the city and county fire departments, a number of churches, the Islamic center, and other emergency service agencies. "Our mindset was, it wasn't about us; it was about how we could help," says Kozlowski. "[We felt] let's establish these relationships and then follow up in any way we can." Staff made phone calls and went into the community to meet with people, and building those community connections yielded unexpected but pleasant results. For example, the captain of the fire department showed museum staff heart-wrenching photographs of local firemen and firewomen, which encouraged the museum to create a display focused on local firefighters.

Many community members had been wondering what activities would be appropriate for the first anniversary of such a terrible event. Several suggestions had been offered, but no decisions had been made; then someone suggested convening a large-scale meeting to discuss everyone's efforts. Eastman House staff offered the museum as a venue, saying, "Let's set up a community meeting to hear what's going on and [guide our own] efforts," recalls Kozlowski.

The George Eastman House's community dialogue—convened to establish a shared understanding about the planning for Sept. 11, 2002—took place on July 20, 2002. Invitations were made by phone and in person, and resulted in a strong turnout. Twenty community leaders attended, including representatives from the corporate sector and the media. Another 15 cited conflicts, but expressed strong interest in being kept informed. Museum staff began the dialogue by presenting their idea for the exhibition of classic images from the Eastman House collections, which would be expanded to include photographs from the community. Others enthusiastically supported the idea and pledged their help. After the meeting, people continued send reports to the museum about what was happening in and around the community.

"The message we worked to convey at the community dialogue was 'Use us; we are planning to be open and free,'" says Kozlowski. "'If there is anything you would like to do here let us know.'" It turned out that representatives of the Islamic Center of Rochester; Jewish Community Federation; Center for Interfaith Study and Dialogue, St. John Fisher College; and the Rochester Interfaith Forum, among other organizations, had been looking for an appropriate venue for an interfaith memorial service planned for the evening of Sept. 11, 2002. This remembrance service and candlelight vigil would include an interfaith choir and biographies of the Sept. 11 victims attached by ribbon to 3,056 candles, one for each person who died in the attacks. One site had been offered, but people thought its location in the more privileged part of the city made it unattractive. Someone suggested the convention center, but others found it too dark and impersonal. However, all were agreed on one point: the museum—a multidimensional gathering place—was ideal.

The decision was made to move the service outdoors to the large expansive lawn at Eastman House. The museum promised to stay open late, allowing attendees to seek solace by walking around the gardens; view a documentary titled *Under Ground Zero*, or meet and talk with one another. Offers of help came from a variety of organizations, including the local Red Cross, which provided volunteers and also trained museum volunteers to handle any emotional outbursts that might occur during the service.

Continuing the Dialogue

The conversations between the staff of the George Eastman House and community members are ongoing. The museum's goal is to explore potential collaborations with each group and to update community stakeholders about the Sept. 11, 2002, events. New partnerships continue to result from these efforts. "We have become the center for the community for any Sept. 11 events," says Kozlowski. "The feedback we are getting is this is exactly what the community needs right now."

And what about the museum's initial idea—the photography exhibit co-curated by the community? "Picturing What Matters: An Offering of Photographs" has developed into a multi-layered exhibition showcasing the personal photographs of members of the community. The museum invited all of Rochester to send in old or new photographs that represented their values, hopes, or dreams. Local print and broadcast media helped get the word out, and a bank placed the call for submissions in all of its branches. Information also was distributed to all 126 local fire houses and all local police patrol sections, as well as numerous other sites throughout the community. As a result, thousands of images were received, and all of them were displayed in the show, on view from Sept. 7, 2002, through Jan. 20, 2003. The Rochester Red Cross was so impressed with the museum's efforts, it invited families of the victims to submit a photograph and/or visit the exhibit.

"This effort, 'Picturing What Matters,' was very healing," says Kozlowski. "It was a chance to look at how our values have been strengthened or changed by these terrible events." It also was a wonderful opportunity to make new friends. "The whole process was so inspiring," she says.

M&C DIALOGUE DEFINITIONS

. . . .

These definitions were compiled to facilitate the dialogue process during AAM's Museums & Community Initiative.

What is a museum?

Most definitions agree on the following characteristics—a museum must:

- be a legally organized not-for-profit institution or part of a not-for-profit institution or government entity;
- be essentially educational in nature;
- have a formally stated mission;
- have a staff member (paid or unpaid) who has museum knowledge and experience and is delegated authority and allocated sufficient financial resources to operate the museum effectively;
- present regularly scheduled programs and exhibits that use and interpret objects for the public according to accepted standards;
- have a formal and appropriate program of documentation, care, and use of collections and/or tangible objects;
- have a formal and appropriate program of presentation and maintenance of exhibits.

- A community is a set of people bound together by common interests, goals, problems or practices. (Adapted from University of St. Gallen (Switzerland) professor Beat F. Schmidt's definition in the glossary of the Net Academy on Media Management; www.mediamanagement.org)

- Community . . . usually refers to (1) a group sharing a defined physical space or geographic area such as a neighborhood, city, village, or hamlet; [or] (2) a group sharing common traits, a sense of belonging, and/or maintaining social ties and interactions which shape it into a distinctive social entity, such as an ethnic, religious, academic or professional community.
(Victor Azarya, sociologist, The Hebrew University of Jerusalem; www.learnativity.com/community.html)

- "Community" means different things to different people. We speak of the community of nations, the community of Jamaica Plain, the gay community, the IBM community, the Catholic community, the Yale community, the African-American community, the "virtual" community of cyberspace, and so on. Each of us derives some sense of belonging from among the various communities to which we might, in principle, belong. (Robert D. Putnam, *Bowling Alone: The Collapse and Revival of American Community*, Simon & Schuster, 2000)

- Community is something more than the sum of the parts, its individual members. What is this "something more"? Even to begin to answer that, we enter a realm that is not so much more abstract as almost mythical. . . . The analogy of a gem comes to mind. . . . A group becomes a community in somewhat the same way that a stone becomes a gem— through a process of cutting and polishing. Once cut and polished, this is something beautiful. But to describe its beauty, the best we can do is to describe its facets. Community, like a gem, is multifaceted, each facet a mere aspect of a whole that defies description. (M. Scott Peck, *The Different Drum: Community-making and Peace*, Touchstone Books, 1998)

What   is   a   livable   community?

A livable community is one that

- stimulates the physical, mental, and spiritual potential of individuals;
- fosters good schools, jobs, housing, public transportation, clean air, and safety;
- encourages a harmonious relationship between man and nature;
- helps conserve energy and natural resources;
- brings quality to the physical, social, economic, and cultural environment;
- encourages a variety of choices, and opportunities (balance) among new and old, large and small, intensive and quiet, communal and private;
- takes advantage of its unique features—climate, geography, population, history, industry—and expresses them through design;
- understands a community's roots;
- develops a participatory attitude to involve people in the planning and use of projects.

. . . What makes a community livable is the people who live in it, their pride in local assets and their willingness to work to preserve them. Ultimately, livability is an attitude, a state of mind, an approach to community. (*Towards Livable Communities, A Report by Partners for Livable Communities*; www.livable.com)

What   is   civic   dialogue?

A dialogue in which people participate in public discussion about civic issues, policies, or decisions of consequence to their lives, communities, and society. . . . The focus of civic dialogue is not about the process of dialogue itself. Nor is its intent solely therapeutic or to nurture personal growth. Rather, civic dialogue addresses a matter of . . . importance to the dialogue participants. Civic dialogue works toward common understanding in an open-ended discussion. It engages multiple perspectives on an issue, including potentially conflicting and unpopular ones, rather than promot[es] a single point of view. (Americans for the Arts, Animating Democracy Initiative, www.artsusa.org/animatingdemocracy/story/index.asp)

What is civic engagement?

Individual and collective actions designed to identify and address issues of public concern. Civic engagement can take many forms, from individual voluntarism to organizational involvement to electoral participation. It can include efforts to directly address an issue, work with others in a community to solve a problem, or interact with institutions of representative democracy. (Michael Delli Carpini, Director, Public Policy, The Pew Charitable Trusts; www.apa.org/ed/slce/civicengagement.html)

What is a civic institution?

One in which the importance of defining and engaging the community has been endorsed as a core value and incorporated into its mission, programs, and practice. Staff, board members, and volunteers spend time thinking about the impact of their work and the institution's overall activities on the community. A civic institution has identified its assets and has determined how they might be linked with the those of other organizations for mutual benefit. Such an institution strives to make its processes, decision-making, and actions open, available, and understandable to the its community.

What is social capital?

Social capital can be defined simply as a . . . set of informal values or norms shared among members of a group that permits them to cooperate with one another. If members of the group come to expect that others will behave reliably and honestly, then they will come to trust one another. Trust acts like a lubricant that makes any group or organization run more effectively. . . . The norms that produce social capital . . . must substantively include virtues like truth telling, meeting obligations, and reciprocity. (Francis Fukuyama, "Social Capital," in *Culture Matters: How Values Shape Human Progress*, Basic Books, 2000)

What are bonding and bridging social capital?

The terms "bonding" and "bridging" social capital describe ways in which we develop relationships of trust and reciprocity with others—both those who are like us (bonding) and those who are different from us (bridging). Bonding social capital is inward-looking and tends to reinforce exclusive identities and homogenous groups; examples include ethnic fraternal organizations, church-based women's reading groups, and fashionable country clubs. Bridging social capital is outward-looking and encompasses socially diverse groups of people; examples include the civil rights movement, many youth service groups, and ecumenical religious organizations. (Adapted from Robert D. Putnam, *Bowling Alone*; and Ross Gittell and Avis Vidal, *Community Organizing: Building Social Capital as a Development Strategy*, Sage, 1998)

RESOURCES
. . . .

American Association of Museums. *Everyone's Welcome: The Americans with Disabilities Act and Museums.* Edited by John P. S. Salmen. American Association of Museums, 1998.

> A manual to help museum professionals and designers better understand the requirements for the Americans with Disabilities Act (ADA). Its recommendations address concerns for visitors with a range of physical and learning disabilities. Also available, a video called *Everyone's Welcome: Universal Access in Museums.*

―――. *Excellence and Equity: Education and the Public Dimension of Museums.* American Association of Museums, 1992.

> An influential report that affirms museums' public service role and challenges them to reach for their potential as educational institutions.

―――. *Mastering Civic Engagement: A Challenge to Museums.* American Association of Museums, 2002.

> This call to action from AAM's Museums & Community Initiative challenges museums to pursue their potential as active, visible players in community life. An opening essay urges museums to reinvigorate their civic role and purposes and offers guideposts for inquiry and transformation. Other essays and reflections—from museums professionals and community practitioners—offer food for thought on the complex process of changing the terms of engagement between communities and museums.

———. *Museums & Community Initiative*: www.aam-us.org.

> Museums & Community is a national initiative of the AAM Board of Directors that explores the potential for dynamic engagement between American communities and their museums.

———. *Museums in the Life of a City: Strategies for Community Partnerships*. American Association of Museums, 1995.

> How can museums play a larger role in the social fabric of a community? This report on an AAM initiative in Philadelphia outlines the possibilities and the challenges, as well as some strategies for long-term partnerships.

———. *New Visions: Tools for Change in Museums*. American Association of Museums, 1995.

> Interactive tools to help the staff and board members of all types of museums explore new ways of thinking, communicating, and planning to advance the effectiveness of the institution. *New Visions* provides a practical framework for assessing the current status and future directions of the institution, thus maximizing the staff and board's ability to meet the museum's mission and connect with its community.

——— and Smithsonian Institution. *Museums for the New Millennium*. American Association of Museums and Center for Museum Studies, Smithsonian Institution, 1997.

> Proceedings from a symposium organized by the Center for Museum Studies at the Smithsonian Institution. Identifies and then systematically explores many of the challenges and opportunities facing the global museum community today.

Americans for the Arts. *Animating Democracy: The Artistic Imagination as a Force in Civic Dialogue*. Americans for the Arts, 1999; www.americans forthearts.org/AnimatingDemocracy.

> An exploration of projects that have successfully connected the arts and civic dialogue, this publication identifies the tremendous role the arts can play in building and sustaining community.

Archibald, Robert R. *A Place to Remember: Using History to Build Community*. AltaMira Press and American Association for State and Local History, 1999.

An exploration of the intersections of history, memory, and community that illustrates how we are active participants in the past and the role and importance of history in contemporary life. Archibald is president of the Missouri Historical Society, a public historian, and chair of the Museums and Community National Task Force.

———. "The Community and the Museum," *History News* (Association for State and Local History) 56 no. 3 (2001), pp. 6-9.

Drawing upon his vast experience, Archibald eloquently explains why museums should seek deeper engagement with their communities.

Association of Science-Technology Centers. "A Common Vision: ASTC's Equity and Diversity Initiative." *ASTC Dimensions*, January/February 2002.

Written in conjunction with the launching of ASTC's Equity & Diversity Initiative, a five-year plan to diversify science centers, this issue addresses why museums need to look more like their communities and how to work towards this goal. Articles include: "Confronting Demographic Denial: Retaining Relevance in the New Millennium", "Walking the Talk: The Importance of a Diversity Plan" and "A Question of Truth: Dialogue in Action."

Carr, David. "The Promise of Cultural Institutions." Presented at the Conference on the 21st Century Learner, Institute for Museum and Library Services, Washington D.C., Nov. 7-9, 2001; www.imls.gov/whatsnew/current/sp110701-1.htm.

A thoughtful commentary on what cultural institutions can be for the public.

The Center for Civil Society Studies: www.jhu.edu/~ccss.

Part of Johns Hopkins University's Institute for Policy Studies, the center strives to support the "development and effective operation of nonprofit, philanthropic, or 'civil society' organizations" through research and information sharing and by providing opportunities for training.

Chew, Ron. "Toward a Dynamic Model of Exhibition-Making," *Museum News*, November/December 2000, p. 47.

"Museums have yet to imagine how they might more agilely and quickly create new exhibitions that respond to current issues and promote community engagement," writes the author. He challenges museums to take a more responsive, public-centered approach.

Columbia University. *Conducting Your Community Dialogue: A Companion to Building a More United America.* The American Assembly, Columbia University, 2002; www.unitingamerica.org.

> A manual that helps organizations participate in the American Assembly's National Dialogue, a series of community events that address difficult social issues with the goal of uniting Americans. This publication includes a useful framework for holding a community dialogue as well as tips for ensuring a successful dialogue.

Community Arts Network (CAN): www.communityartsnetwork.net.

> CAN is a partnership between Art in the Public Interest (www.apionline.org) and the Virginia Tech Department of Theatre Arts' Consortium for the Study of Theatre and Community. It provides the "information exchange, research, and critical dialogue within the field of community-based arts." Includes a virtual reading room, where visitors can browse by subject area.

Fukuyama, Francis. *Trust: The Social Virtues and the Creation of Prosperity.* Free Press, 1995; Touchstone Books, 1996.

> In *Trust*, Fukuyama examines the role of social capital—reciprocity, moral obligation, duty toward community, and trust"—in facilitating the "stability and prosperity of post-industrial societies."

Gates, Christopher T. "Democracy & The Civic Museum." *Museum News*, May/June 2001.

> What role will museums play in the reinvention of our democracy?

Gladwell, Malcolm. *The Tipping Point: How Little Things Can Make a Big Difference.* Little Brown & Company, 2000.

> How can we successfully promote an agenda and create the "magic moment when an idea, trend, or social behavior crosses a threshold, tips and spreads like wildfire?"

Harrison, Lawrence E., and Samuel P. Huntington, eds. *Culture Matters: How Values Shape Human Progress.* Basic Books, 2000.

> Essays and presentations from a symposium organized by Harvard University's Academy for International and Area Studies that consider the role of culture (in its broadest sense) in the development of economic and social progress.

Harvard University. *Better Together: Report of the Saguaro Seminar on Civic Engagement in America.* John F. Kennedy School of Government, Harvard University, 2000; www.bettertogether.org.

A report from the Saguaro Seminar, a multiyear dialogue that focuses on how we can build bonds of civic trust among Americans and their communities. One chapter deals with the arts and social capital.

Hirzy, Ellen, Kim Igoe, and Alexandra Marmion Roosa. "Listening to the Voices in Our Communities," *Journal of Museum Education* (Museum Education Roundtable) 27, no. 3. (summer 2002).

What did AAM hear during its six M&C Dialogues? This article provides a useful summary of the participants' responses.

ICOM Canada. "Museums and Sustainability," *ICOM Canada Bulletin,* April 2000; www.chin.gc.ca/Resources/Icom/English/e_apr_00.html.

Five articles exploring museums' role in sustainable development.

Institute of Museum and Library Services. *A Closer Look.* Institute of Museum and Library Services; www.imls.gov/closer.

Regularly updated highlights from IMLS-funded projects, often focusing on community engagement.

McCarthy, Kevin, and Kimberly Jannett. *A New Framework for Building Participation in the Arts.* RAND, 2001.

Arts organizations across the country are expanding their efforts to increase public participation in their programs. This report presents the findings of a RAND study of these efforts, the purpose of which was two-fold: to better understand the process by which individuals become involved in the arts and to identify how arts institutions can most effectively influence that process.

Museum Education Roundtable. "The Museum as a Public Place," *Journal of Museum Education* 24, nos. 1 and 2 (1999).

What does it mean to be a public place? What are the features of a vital public place, and what are the implications for museums? Articles include "The Civic Museum: A Place in the World," "Museums and Livable Communities," and "Space Creatures: The Museum as Urban Intervention and Social Forum."

Museum Loan Network. *Museum as Catalyst for Interdisciplinary Collaboration: Beginning a Conversation.* Museum Loan Network, 2002.

> What are some of the challenges and opportunities for interdisciplinary collaboration? What roles can museums and their collections play? Findings from a series of meetings convened by the Museum Loan Network.

National Civic League: www.ncl.org.

> Headquartered in Denver, the National Civic League is a 107-year-old nonprofit, non-partisan organization dedicated to strengthening civic democracy by transforming democratic institutions.

Program for Community Problem Solving: www.ncl.org/NCL/pcps.htm.

> A national organization that works directly with communities to foster cross-sector collaboration and grassroots problem-solving.

New York Foundation for the Arts. *Culture Counts: Strategies for a More Vibrant Cultural Life for New York City.* New York Foundation for the Arts, 2001.

> This landmark report from A Cultural Blueprint for New York City, a special initiative of the New York Foundation of the Arts, is the first comprehensive study of cultural life in New York City in 30 years. Included are the first-ever survey of New Yorkers' participation in arts and culture activities and organizations, including museums, and a series of findings and recommendations related to public-policy decision-making in the city.

Oldenburg, Ray. *The Great Good Place: Cafés, Coffee Shops, Bookstores, Bars, Hair Salons, and other Hangouts at the Heart of a Community*, 2d ed. Marlow and Co., 1999.

> A vision for the revitalization of "third places"—the public places where people can gather, put aside the concerns of home and work, and hang out simply for the pleasures of good company and lively conversation. Oldenburg argues that these settings of informal public life are essential for the health of individuals and communities.

Pew Charitable Trusts. *Program for Art Museums and Communities*: www. artmusecomm.org.

> Eleven art museums that are strengthening community alliances and

exploring new programming approaches. To access ArtConText, the project from the Rhode Island School of Design Museum, go to: www.risd.edu/artcontext/index.htm.

Pew Partnerships for Civic Change: A Spotlight on Solutions: www.pew-partnership.org.

> The Pew Partnership is a civic research organization whose mission is to identify, document, and disseminate promising solutions for creating strong communities, i.e., thriving neighborhoods, living-wage jobs, viable economies, healthy families and children, and collaborative leadership. The Partnership's research explores how innovative partnerships, citizen participation, and accessible technology can lead to civic solutions in those five areas. Funded by the Pew Charitable Trusts and administered by the University of Richmond.

Putnam, Robert D. *Bowling Alone: The Collapse and Revival of American Community*. Simon & Schuster, 2000.

> A comprehensive assessment of community life in American that examines the rise and fall of social organizations, civic groups, and organized religion over the last century. The author is well known for an essay that appeared a few years before the book's publication, which speculated on the reasons for and meaning behind the simultaneous increase in individual bowlers and sharp decline of bowling leagues.

Strom, Elizabeth. *Strengthening Communities through Culture*. The Center for Arts & Culture, 2001; www.culturalpolicy.org.

> The third issue paper from Art, Culture, and the National Agenda, a project of the Center for Arts and Culture, examines the crucial link between culture and vibrant communities.

The Study Circles Resource Center, www.studycircles.org.

> This national organization is devoted to community-wide dialogue on a range of contemporary issues.

Thelen, David. "Learning Community: Lessons in Co-Creating the Civic Museum," *Museum News*, May/June 2001.

> Insightful comments, based on the author's observations of the M&C dialogues, on the promise and problems associated with the development of the civic museum.

The Urban Institute: www.urban.org.

A non-partisan research center that creates and disseminates publishes studies, reports, and books on important issues affecting the public.

Yankelovich, Daniel. *The Magic of Dialogue: Transforming Conflict into Cooperation.* Touchstone Books, 2001.

Yankelovich offers strategies to help individuals develop the necessary competencies for engaging in successful dialogues.

MUSEUMS & COMMUNITY PROJECT TEAM

. . . .

Edward H. Able, Jr., president & CEO, AAM

Robert R. Archibald, Ph.D., president and CEO, Missouri Historical Society, St. Louis, and chair, Museums & Community Initiative National Task Force

Kim Igoe, project director, Museums & Community, and vice president, policy & programs, AAM

Patricia E. Williams, former project director, Museums & Community, and vice president & chief operating officer, Americans for the Arts, Washington, D.C.

Ingrid Denis, former program associate, policy & programs, AAM

Ellen Hirzy, consulting writer, Museums & Community

Jerold D Kappel, director of development, AAM

Jane Lusaka, editor, Museums & Community, and assistant director, publications, AAM

Maureen Robinson, project consultant and dialogue facilitator, Museums & Community

Alexandra Marmion Roosa, project manager, Museums & Community

David Thelen, observer/evaluator, Museums & Community, and professor of history, Indiana University, Bloomington